# MEDITATION FOR BEGINNERS

## OVERCOME ANXIETY, RELIEVE STRESS, FIGHT DEPRESSION, CONQUER FEAR, FIND INNER PEACE, HAPPINESS, MINDFULNESS

*BY SMART READS*

## Free Audiobook

As a thank you for being a Smart Reader you can choose 2 FREE audiobooks from audible.com. Simply sign up for free by visiting www.audibletrial.com/Travis to get your books.

## Visit:

www.smartreads.co/freebooks

to receive Smart Reads books for FREE

## Check us out on Instagram:

www.instagram.com/smart_readers

@smart_readers

# ABOUT SMARTREADS

Choose Smart Reads and get smart every time. Smart Reads sorts through all the best content and condenses the most helpful information into easily digestible chunks.

We design our books to be short, easy to read and highly informative. Leaving you with maximum understanding in the least amount of time.

Smart Reads aims to accelerate the spread of quality information so we've taken the copyright off everything we publish and donate our material directly to the public domain. You can read our uncopyright below.

We believe in paying it forward and donate 5% of our net sales to Pencils of Promise to build schools, train teachers and support child education.

To limit our footprint and restore forests around the globe we are planting a tree for every 10 hardcover books we sell.

Thanks for choosing Smart Reads and helping us help the planet.

Sincerely,

Travis & the Smart Reads Team

# TABLE OF CONTENTS

# INTRODUCTION

When it comes to living today, no one can deny that life has become a lot more stressful – we are living in a world where we are connected 24/7 and our brains are pounded by stimuli on a constant basis – down time is busier than ever before and we are never truly out of reach anymore.

Is it any wonder then that so many of us feel shell-shocked? We are running ourselves ragged trying to keep up - with work and with our social lives. Being stressed out is seen as a badge of honor rather than a situation that needs to be resolved.

Are you feeling wrecked? Are you tired of being on the go all the time? Longing to just run away from it all? Well, this book is for you. This book will show you how to restore calm and balance in your life in just a few minutes a day – and it's not going to involve quitting your job to join an ashram or to buy expensive props.

In as little as 5 minutes a day, meditation can change your life. And once you get the hang of it, it is unbelievably simple to do.

Here, you'll learn the benefits of meditation and how you can meditate yourself. This book will guide you through a few easy meditation practices and then detail a few of the different types of meditations so you can choose the style that suits you best.

Once you follow the steps, you can restore the calm in your own world and become your own guru. Ready to feel the calm? Let's get started!

# CHAPTER 1: MEDITATION AND HOW IT AFFECTS YOUR MIND

We all know that what we think has a strong influence on how we feel. When we think of something sad, we feel sad, when we think of something that upsets us, we feel angry. It stands to reason then that controlling what we think is the first step in controlling how we feel.

The problem is that controlling what we are thinking can be a lot more difficult than it sounds originally, especially when it comes to worrying or feeling down.

**Thoughts Create Your Reality**
Henry Ford once said, "Whether you think you can, or think you can't, you're right."

If you are unable to rein in feelings of being sad, anxious or depressed, you are going to find yourself caught in a vicious cycle – you will be unable to accomplish what you want because you are too depressed or anxious and then you become more depressed or anxious because of your lack of accomplishment.

Now, while it is natural for everyone to feel this way occasionally, being constantly mired down by these feelings is far from natural and creates in us a state of ill-health that makes it difficult to function in the real world.

We become more and more depressed, unable to move on from these feelings and finding more confirmation of everything that happens around you. The simple fact is that when you feel bad, you are likely to notice bad things happening in the world around you and in turn, makes you feel worse, making it likely that bad things will happen to you.

The contrary is also true – when you feel good, you are likely to notice good things around you and this makes you feel better, making it likely that good things will happen to you.

But when depression or anxiety is out of control, things go a step further as well. Instead of worrying about what has gone wrong, dealing with it and moving on, we keep mulling it over. And then, as if to add insult to injury, the mind starts to worry about things that have not happened yet and will most likely not happen at all.

What does end up happening once you reach this point is that you spend your life in a state of constant anxiety and depression, feeling nothing will ever go right for you again. The good news is that you can start training your mind to behave differently. It is not always going to be easy, but if you need to gain control of your mind, meditation is the tool that you will need to do so.

Meditating to Break the Cycle of Negative Thought
There are several types of meditation, all of which involve concentrating on the here and now, rather than on the future or the past. Meditation is also extremely useful if you need to break out of negative programming.

Meditation helps you to center the mind and body. You are basically training your mind to control what it is thinking and this can be useful when not meditating as well. You can literally learn to stop focusing on negative thoughts and learn to channel more positive ones instead.

# CHAPTER 2: THE BENEFITS OF MEDITATION

Now that you understand how meditation can help you to overcome negative thinking. Let's go through all the benefits of meditation.

**The Physical Benefits**
Meditation has a profound effect on the whole body. It helps induce a state of deep relaxation and, as a result, you will find that:

• Your blood pressure becomes lower
• The levels of stress hormones in the blood stream become reduced, helping to reduce inflammation and thus making you healthier.
• You become calmer and less anxious on a daily basis
• Physical symptoms related to tension like insomnia, headaches, muscular aches and pains, ulcers and problems with joint mobility are reduced.
• Meditation causes an increase in the production of serotonin and this helps you to feel better and more able to cope.
• It boosts the action of the immune system.
• It helps you to better channel your internal energy so you feel more important.

## Mental Benefits

Meditation helps to slow the mind and put it into the healing Alpha state. Neuroscientists have learned that the mind physically starts to reshape itself after regular sessions and this can have lasting effects on your health and well-being.

- Your overall levels of anxiety decrease.
- Your moods become more even.
- You become more creative.
- You feel happier and more at peace.
- You become more intuitive.
- Your brain's ability to focus improves and you are better able to see things clearly.
- Problems faced seem less overwhelming in general.

## Spiritual Benefits

- You are better able to connect with the divine.
- You will find yourself transforming at a personal level.
- Sound meditation – chanting a specific sound – can be very effective at clearing blockages in the chakras or the body's energy centers. The sounds resonate and thus help to restore balance in the body's systems.

Regularly practicing meditation allows you to clear out unnecessary thoughts and feelings and allows you to focus your mind so it's calmer and less agitated. It helps you to concentrate and cut through the myriad of distractions and start working through all the experiences in your life that have caused you stress. You will be able to analytically delve into these experiences and identify patterns in your behavior that may have led you to those moments, thus allowing you to identify those patterns and, where necessary, reducing the stress associated with them overall.

Spiritually, as you begin to delve deeper and deeper into your meditation sessions, you will find issues that might have been plaguing you for years are properly dealt with and you begin to see things in a whole new light. The advantage of working through these experiences, no matter how painful they are, is that you become more centered and have more room to start enjoying other emotions such as love and joy. The key to seeing these benefits is to be consistent in your efforts to meditate. Try to set aside time every day or every other day to do this. As time passes, you will start to find that you actually start looking forward to your meditation sessions and actively look for opportunities to meditate.

If you are still not convinced about how important meditation is, try this exercise:

Sit in a comfortable position and breathe in deeply and slowly a few times. Once you are more relaxed, stop thinking – just sit and stare at a point on the wall or try humming a tune – whatever it takes to still your mind. Just still your mind for 5 minutes.

Afterwards, think about it for a few minutes – how well did it work for you? What would have happened if it had been for a longer period of time? How did your brain react when you told it to stop thinking? The brain is rebellious in nature – I am willing to bet that just telling it to stop thinking was not enough and perhaps even caused it to think even more.

The good news is that with practice, you can train your brain to be more of a team player.

# CHAPTER 3: GETTING STARTED

Meditation has been a practice in many different cultures for centuries and has been practiced by millions of people. As a result, it should not come as a surprise that there are many different types of meditation and ways to achieve a meditative state. While this makes it easier to customize and find the right meditation techniques to suit you, it can be terribly confusing when you're just starting out.

Meditation is simply a form of deep state of concentration. You concentrate on an object or a word or even your breath and exclude all other thoughts. It is best to start out by concentrating on one tangible thing as this makes it easier to still the mind overall. As you become more accomplished, you can switch over to meditating on more intangible things – such as a picture in your mind's eye as opposed to a physical thing or word.

In the first few meditations, just concentrate on your breathing and not worry too much about chanting or anything else.

**Your First Meditation Exercise**
Sit comfortably in an area where you will not be disturbed – somewhere peaceful and quiet. Switch

your mobile phone off completely. Make sure you are wearing non-restrictive clothing and that you are sitting comfortably in whatever position you find comfortable.

If you are worried that you might over-meditate, then set a timer for 15 minutes or so. Just ensure it is not one of those ticking timers as this can end up distracting you as well.

Close your eyes and breathe in slowly to the count of four. Hold the breath for a count of 4 and then release slowly to the count of four. While doing this, concentrate only on your breathing. If your mind wanders, gently move your attention back to your breathing and concentrate on the count.

**Start Now**

Now that you have a basic meditation process to follow, you can simply start. Don't get too caught up in the preparation that you sacrifice time that would be better spent meditating.

Check your schedule and your home and choose a time and place for you to meditate. If you need to adjust your schedule a bit or if you need to make the room more conducive to meditating – by putting in a timer, for example, or setting out some comfortable cushions, do so now.

Now that your space is ready and you have set up your schedule, you are ready to start on this journey. Sit down and start, clearing your mind of all expectations. Look at meditation more like an essential part of living – something that needs to be done on a daily basis and something that puts no additional pressure on you to succeed.

So many people expect to come out of their first meditation completely relaxed and enlightened without realizing that meditation is a long-term solution, not a quick stop gap measure.
You will start to feel a bit more relaxed from the first meditation onwards but do not try to push this process too much or you will have problems.

## Plumbing the Depths of Your Soul
Right now, as a beginner, there is no need to worry about soul searching or digging too deeply when it comes to meditation.

This will come, eventually, when you are more practiced at the art of meditation and there is no need to rush yourself to that point before you are ready.

You don't need to meditate about "deep" subjects such as the meaning of life.

# CHAPTER 4: SIMPLE MEDITATIONS TO GET YOU STARTED

Meditation practice doesn't need to be too complex – as mentioned before; it is whatever works for you. For beginners, it is better to start out with simple exercises and try to maintain concentration over shorter periods of time, at least at first. Five to ten minutes may not seem long but when you are dealing with clearing the mind it can be.

It is also advisable to try a few different techniques to see which work best for you overall. In this chapter, we will go through some simple meditations in different styles so you can get a feel for meditation as a whole.

**A Basic Relaxation Exercise**
This is an exercise that is good to perform when your body is particularly tense. It only takes a few minutes and fits in right before your meditation.

Sit comfortably and close your eyes. Breathe in deeply and clench your feet for a few seconds. Relax them and feel the tension melting away. Repeat this procedure with your calves and then thigh muscles, moving your way all the way up your body and arms and ending with the muscles in your face.

Repeat if necessary.

This exercise helps to drain muscle aches from the body as a whole.

## A Meaningful Meditation

Find yourself a place to meditate, one where you will be undisturbed for at least 15 minutes. Switch off your phone and any other loud noises in the room. You can, if you like, play relaxing music to aid you in quieting the mind. It is best if it is a soft background noise and music that has no lyrics. Identify a phrase that has some meaning to you – this will be your mantra during the meditation. For example, "Love is key."

Sit comfortably in a relaxed posture but do ensure that your back is straight. If your body is tense, you are going to need to do the basic relaxation exercise detailed above.

Close your eyes and breathe in deeply through your nose, all the time repeating the phrase that you chose in your head. It is important, for this exercise to ensure that you only repeat the phrase in your head and not out loud. (There are meditations that involve chanting but this is not one of them.)

Hold your breath for a count of five, and then release slowly through the mouth, again repeating your chosen phrase silently to yourself. Repeat this a few times and then finish off by concentrating on your breathing overall. Then slowly bring yourself back into things by opening your eyes and getting up slowly. Give yourself a minute or two before you go back to your normal day.

It is important, in the beginning at least, to do a basic review of how things went. This doesn't need to be a major analysis, just a quick check to figure out if this method worked for you. Was it easy to concentrate on your phrase or did your mind wander quite a bit? Was it easy to remember your phrase or did you keep having to think what it was?

Do not be too upset if this first meditation didn't work as you had hoped it would. This is something that you need to practice. This meditation will also not work for everyone; so do experiment with the others as well until you get the hang of things.

**Some Basic Transcendental Meditation**
Get comfortable in a place where you will be undisturbed. In this exercise, you will choose an object to concentrate on. You can, for example, concentrate on the flame of a candle or a specific spot on the wall. It is best to choose a fairly generic item that will not evoke too much of an emotional response. (You can,

once you have the hang of things, progress to an object that has more meaning to you.)

Relax and start to breathe in slowly through your nose and out through your mouth. Concentrate on the item that you have chosen. If thoughts come to mind, let them pass without judgment, always returning your focus to the object that you chose.

Maintain this for a few minutes and then gradually allow your focus to shift back to everyday life. Give yourself a few minutes to get back to full consciousness again and then evaluate the success of the exercise as a whole. Again, do not worry if it did not work out exactly as you hoped it would.

**Meditation through Breathing**
Sit in a comfortable position where you will be undisturbed. In this exercise, you will concentrate on your breath as well but this time there will be no counting involved. You will simply act as an observer, noting how the breath moves in through the nostrils, fills out your lungs and pushes out your belly. In this exercise, you simply allow the breathing to occur in its own natural rhythm without forcing it one way or another.

If you find that your mind wanders, gently refocus your attention on your breathing again. Thoughts and images will almost certainly continue to keep coming up as you try to calm your mind but that is nothing to worry about – simply push them to the back of your mind again and refocus on your breath. Keep coming back to your breath. If you find that this is too difficult to maintain, do the Basic Meditation exercise in Chapter 2, counting your breaths. If focusing on the breathing rather than the counting does not work at first, try it again in a few weeks' time. It may be that all your brain really needs in order to focus is some practice in meditation.

**Deep Relaxation**
Here's a meditation you can do any time you have a little bit longer to spend on the meditation or if you want to really get rid of the stress and tension that accumulates over the course of daily life. This is a great exercise for you to do when you feel that you need to relax and recharge a bit.

Dress comfortably in non-constricting clothes and lie down flat. The floor is the ideal place for this exercise as the bed may be too comfortable. You need to place your arms loosely at your sides and position your legs a little apart from one another.

Take a few seconds to feel the sensation of your body touching the floor and sensing where you are carrying tension in your body.

Close your eyes and breathe in deeply through your nose. While you are breathing in, concentrate on your feet. As you breathe out, wriggle your feet a bit, making sure to alternate flexing and pointing. Relax your feet. As you do so, feel the tension flowing out of them into the floor. Your feet will start to feel lighter and lot more relaxed.

Repeat this exercise with your calves, then your thighs and then your hips, all the while imagining the tension and any pain present flowing out of your limbs and into the floor with every exhalation.

Move up to the belly and take a few deep breathes, again imagining the tension flowing out of your belly and into the floor.

Repeat with the chest and neck before moving onto the shoulders, arms and hands. Throughout this whole process, the areas that are relaxed should start to feel very light.

Finish off by concentrating on doing the same for your head. If you can, imagine the tension dripping off your scalp as well.

End off by checking each area again for any leftover tension, repeating the exercise as necessary in those areas where there is still some tension.

Now concentrate on the feeling of complete relaxation as you imagine your whole body becoming light and relaxed. Lay in that pose for about 5 minutes, concentrating on the feelings of relaxation.

If you start to feel bored, it is time to call it quits. Bring yourself out of it by moving your hands and feet again and stretching your limbs thoroughly. Once that is done you can open your eyes and sit up slowly. Stretch again thoroughly before standing and, once you are up, stretch one last time.

**Sound Meditation**
With this meditation, you will choose a mantra or sound that appeals to you and follow the same basic steps as those used in Meaningful Meditation. The difference here is that you will say the sound out loud. It is best to choose a simple sound or mantra like "Om" or "Love is key." Choose something that resonates with you.

**Prayer Beads Meditation**

This is a form of meditation that has proven very effective across both Eastern and Western cultures. Do not be put off by the name, "prayer beads" as this is simply a term used. You can look for a rosary or worry beads if you like or even just get a string of beads – it really doesn't matter what size and shape as long as they are of even size and strung in a continuous strand – no clasps or fastenings.

For this meditation, you simply hold the beads in your dominant hand and, as you are repeating your mantra (in your head or out loud), you run each bead through your fingers. The beads help to keep your mind occupied a bit and make it easier to clear your mind of thoughts other than your mantra.

You can, if you like, choose a set that has one bead that is slightly smaller than the others or that has a marked beginning and end to help you mark time.

**Clear Your Mind Meditation**

This is another good exercise if you want to clear your mind of all thought and just find some calm in the chaos.

Sit comfortably and close your eyes. Take a few deep breaths and visualize a huge white screen in your mind's eye. This screen should take up the whole field of "vision." I imagine a movie theater screen since that works really well.

Now imagine a black dot forming in the center of the screen. Imagine it increasing in size until it takes up the whole screen and the white area is completely replaced by the black dot.

Again, focus on the screen, this time imagining a white dot in the center of it. Now imagine the white dot growing and growing until it completely covers the whole of the black screen.

Repeat this a few times over in order to completely clear your mind.

# CHAPTER 5: MINDFULNESS MEDITATION

All meditation does is focus your mind on one particular activity, rather than having a bunch of thoughts whizzing through it. Sometimes you simply do not have the time to sit and formally meditate but there are still ways to fit a form of meditation into your daily schedule. Mindfulness meditation can be done anywhere, anytime and involves simply paying complete attention to the task at hand. That means that you focus on the here and now, giving your task your complete attention rather than allowing your mind to go on autopilot and your thoughts with it. Your mind is like a little child at times – it becomes easily bored and wants to find other things to occupy itself. How often have you driven or ridden to work and gotten there without actually remembering the trip? It's likely you've done this so many times without even realizing it.

Changing the Focus of Your Attention Inward
The problem with living on autopilot or not concentrating on the task at hand is you end up missing a chunk of the present. Perhaps you are too concerned with what is going on around you, perhaps your thoughts have turned to the future – whatever the distraction is, it is preventing you from living in the present moment and this is a real shame. You are

so focused on external stimuli or things that haven't happened that you forget about how you are feeling in the here and now. This makes the attainment of happiness impossible to achieve.

We are taught that happiness is something we must find externally, something we must chase by having a plan for the future. In truth, the key to being happy is in each and every one of us.

Do this exercise really quickly – think about what you are feeling at this moment in time – what are your thoughts, what sensations are you experiencing? Is it hard to move your focus inwards or to concentrate on what your senses are telling you?

If you found this exercise difficult, you are not alone. Your mind is like a naughty little child, wanting to do only what it wants to do and getting bored quickly and easily. It will try to distract you by sending more thoughts your way and, as a result, it may be difficult to simply concentrate on what is happening in the here and now only.

This constant state of flux is what the brain has become used to throughout the years and so you will need to be patient and just keep coming back to focusing on the present moment and what you are feeling and sensing. With regular practice, you will become more adept at the process overall and you can unlearn the habit of always thinking a few steps ahead. There are several different variations of this exercise so choose one of these if they work better for you.

**Variation 1:**
Focus merely on what you are thinking, sensing and feeling and how experiencing it actually changes the overall experience. You might, for example, notice how your brain moves from one thought to the next or even that you are thinking. Instead of worrying about what the thoughts mean, you could observe simply that you are feeling things.

**Variation 2:**
You will need to overcome the brain's tendency to focus on external stimuli and instead focus on your own internal experience. When you get the hang of things, you can switch this out again and focus on the external rather than the internal world.

**Variation 3:**
Here you will ignore any thoughts on the past or future and concentrate on the experience that you are having at the moment. It does not matter if you have done the same thing over and over again, each new time is different and focusing on what you are

experiencing now rather than what you have experienced in the past will make this very clear to you.

**Variation 4:**
When you got out of bed this morning, what were your first thoughts? I do not doubt that you thought about everything that you had to accomplish today, running through your mental to do list. We all have lists of things that we need to be doing and so we end up doing things rather than simply being. Remember when you were a child and you simply took life as it came? Try to get back into that state of being, rather than worrying about what it is that you have to do.

**Total Relaxation**
When you first start meditating, you will have some kinks that need to be ironed out. You have no doubt accumulated a lot of stress and tension in your body over the years and this can be difficult to get rid of. By meditating, you are taking the focus away from these stresses and tensions and allowing yourself to forget about them for at least a short time. Over time, these benefits accumulate and you start to see a noticeable improvement in stress and tension in the body.

In the beginning, though, this state of deep relaxation may be hard to come by and so I have included some meditations that you can do at any time to help both mind and body.

**Walking Meditation**
If you are too restless to sit and meditate, you can engage in a walking meditation. This is a type of meditation that is widely practiced and has been revered throughout the centuries. It is the concept behind this that led to the development of meditation labyrinths. Basically, the labyrinth is set up as a path that must be followed, with a complex design. There is only one path to walk on but the labyrinth twists and turns so that the mind cannot figure out how to "beat" it. As a result, the mind gives up trying to figure it out and you simply experience walking the path and being present in that moment. The Chartres Cathedral Labyrinth in France is one of the most famous examples of a meditation labyrinth.

You can consider setting up a smaller model in your backyard or you can simply walk backwards and forwards inside or outside your home – it depends on what you prefer and are comfortable with.
Start off by walking as normal and counting your breathing as you go along. Once you have established the rhythm, you can start to alter your steps in line

with your breathing. You might, for example, inhale to the count of four and take four steps at the same time. You can then exhale to the count of four and take another four steps at the same time. The number of steps is not all that important, as long as you are consistent and keep the same pace throughout.

As you monitor your breathing, you can also take note of the sensation of your feet hitting the ground and your legs moving. Do not look directly at the ground but rather look slightly ahead of you.

It may be difficult to concentrate on both your breathing and the sensation of your legs and feet moving and if you are finding that, you can choose to concentrate on just one of these aspects until you become more practiced at walking meditations. Whether you are concentrating on the movement itself or breathing or both, do not let your mind wander at all and always bring your attention back to the movement or breathing in the present.

**Mindful Eating**
How do you react to mealtimes? Do you wolf down half the food without even properly tasting it because your mind is focused on other things? Mindful eating can help put a stop to that and benefit you at the same time. You will now take the time to actually taste each

and every mouthful of food, and take the time to acknowledge the sensations of eating.

This will help you to slow down eating and make eating a more pleasurable experience than ever before. It will help to reduce tension and will facilitate proper digestion of the food.

Before tucking in, have a look at the food itself and what has gone into its preparation. Take time to smell the aromas of the food and to enjoy what it tastes like. Take a little time to be thankful for the food on your plate.

When you pick up your knife and fork, concentrate on how it feels to cut the food. When you put the food in your mouth, concentrate on the scents and flavors of the food, how it feels to eat it, what it tastes like and how it feels to swallow it.

Taking time to experience your food rather than wolfing it down will help you to slow down and enjoy your food overall.

**Light Healing Meditation**
This meditation is for being mindful of the body and thus learning which areas are most in need of healing. Start by doing your normal relaxation exercises and begin a normal meditation. After meditating for a few

minutes, breathe in deeply 4 times, each time releasing a bit more tension with every exhalation. Imagine a clear ball of energy and light just ahead of you.

In this light, the qualities that you want to manifest or feel that you need right now are all present. Concentrate on one or two things in this first meditation and imagine them being in the light, being as specific as possible.

As the light hovers in front of you, feel its glow and radiance entering your body and making you feel warmer and more at peace. (I find it helpful to look on the light as gentle sunshine.)

Imagine the ball of energy drawing on the benevolent powers within the universe that will help you to heal and grow.

Imagine your body soaking up the healing energies of this ball of energy and beginning to glow with inner radiance as more and more of the energy is taken in. Visualize the negative energy and tension draining out of your body and being replaced by this wonderful light and the properties that you have determined that you need to draw through to you.

Carry on in this fashion until you have absorbed all the energy from the ball and taken it into yourself. Visualize the energy flooding every cell of your body Continue to imagine this powerful, healing light flooding every cell of your body and you taking on the healing essence yourself.

Meditate on this for a few more minutes before gently bringing yourself out of it again.

**Conscious Smiling**
When you are feeling down, the very act of smiling can help you to feel a little better. The facial muscles are relaxed when you are smiling and this is why real joy has such a healing effect. By forcing yourself to consciously smile, you also present a kinder, gentler face to the world and they respond by being kinder to you. This, in turn, can help you to feel happier and kinder overall as well.

Sit back and relax, practicing some deep breathing and getting into your normal meditation pose.
Now smile a little – it does not have to be a fake grimace; a half smile will work just as well. Identify the feelings that you experience when smiling and whether or not your body relaxes. Do you feel comfortable smiling in this manner or do you feel like a bit of an idiot?

Now that you have practiced smiling during a meditation and have identified the feelings that come with it, you need to incorporate the smiles into your daily life for about 10 minutes at a time. You can choose the time and place that you like – smile over the breakfast table or on the subway, the choice is yours.

After doing this every day for a week, review whether or not smiling has changed the way that you interact with others or how they respond to you.

Continue to incorporate conscious smiling into your life and, the next time that you are feeling blue, hold the smile for a minimum of 30 minutes and see if that does not help you to feel a lot better.

**Peaceful Place**
This meditation is one that draws on your own experience to produce a feeling of calm and relaxation. It is a very effective meditation for those times when you are really feeling stressed out and ill.

Start as you would with any other mediation, taking deep breaths and relaxing the body.

Bring to mind a time that you felt completely at peace and relaxed. A moment in life when you knew that you were safe from harm and felt protected. A safe place that you can picture well in your mind.

Remember the place in as much detail as you possibly can, taking the time to recall the look of the place, the sounds of the place and the aromas present as well. Imagine that you are back there now and enjoying the feel of the air, the light of the sun, if applicable and the feel of ground contacting your skin.

Explore it fully, recalling the feelings associated with that very moment and enjoy being back there once more.
When you are finished, take deep breaths again and start to come out of the meditation

# CHAPTER 6: IMPROVING YOUR MEDITATIVE EXPERIENCE

Aside from consistent practice, there are a few other things that you can do to help to improve your meditative practice.

## Using Mudras

A mudra is basically the position of your arm and hand. Traditionally each of the fingers is connected to a particular element and so holding particular fingers together can help you to change your focus. Here are some simple mudras to start you off:

**Gyan:** This is one of the simplest and most effective of the mudras. It helps reduce tension, depressions, helps to hone focus and is associated with wisdom. Hold together the forefinger and thumb, allowing the other fingers to straighten out and relax.

**Dhyana:** This is useful when you want to lose yourself in thought and can help you to meditate. Place the right hand on top of your left hand and rest on your folded legs. Let the thumbs relax naturally so that a triangle is formed.

## Using Aromatherapy

Diffusing essential oils whilst meditating can be very effective when it comes to maintaining focus and relaxing. Some of the oils you can try include:

• Myrrh for focus and stress relief
• Sandalwood for stress relief and to heal at an emotional and spiritual level
• Rose for connecting with spirit and enhancing happiness
• Vetiver for focusing, grounding and intense relaxation
• Sage for clearing out negativity in the mind, body and the immediate environment.

**Problems You Might Encounter and Dealing with Them**
As I have mentioned before, it is not always easy to learn how to quiet the mind. In this section, you will learn some problems that you may encounter and what you can do to solve these:

• **Impatience:** This is common, especially when you have a lot to do. You might want to do something else or you might be annoyed at yourself because you are not making the progress that you wanted to. To overcome this, do anything that is really urgent before you sit down and meditate. If it is a lack of progress that is worrying you, give yourself a break – no matter how easy it seems when we think of it, actually sitting down to meditate and doing so successfully takes practice.

•　　　**Getting Distracted:** Again, this is very common – it is a tactic the mind often uses so that we can avoid the issue. It is also not the mind's natural state to sit quietly without thinking of anything. When you get distracted, gently pull yourself back to the primary meditation. If it is a continuous problem, try counting your breathing to help remove the distracting thoughts.

•　　　**Getting Bored**: Not all of us are made to do nothing at all. If you find yourself getting bored during the meditation exercises, focus instead on counting your breathing. Over time  you will learn to quiet the mind altogether but it might take some time along with constant practice.

•　　　Unable to control your thoughts: There will be times when you won't be able to control the thoughts that come into your brain. This is perfectly natural and basically means that your subconscious is starting to communicate with you. These may be meaningful thoughts or they may not be, simply allow yourself to think them and then try to refocus again.

# CONCLUSION

By now, you should have a better understanding of how to meditate and at least have tried 2 or 3 of the exercises presented in the book.

If you're still starting out and frustrated at the lack of immediate results, don't be discouraged. Keep trying. When it comes to meditating, you get as many points for effort as you do for results. Keep practicing and trying different methods and you will hit on at least one that seems made for you.

If you're determined to make this practice a part of your life, commit to at least five minutes a day of meditation. If you want to add more time after you get the hang of it, so be it. But all you really need is five minutes a day, each and every day, to change your life forever.

⁇

# THANKS FOR READING

We really hope you enjoyed this book. If you found this material helpful feel free to share it with friends. You can also help others find it by leaving a review where you purchased the book. Your feedback will help us continue to write books you love.

The Smart Reads library is growing by the day! Make sure and check out the other wonderful books in our catalog. We would love to hear which books are your favorite.

**Visit:**
www.smartreads.co/freebooks
to receive Smart Reads books for FREE



**Check us out on Instagram:**
www.instagram.com/smart_readers
@smart_readers



Don't forget your 2 FREE audiobooks.
Use this link www.audibletrial.com/Travis to claim
your 2 FREE Books.

# SMART READS ORIGINS

Smart Reads was born out of the desire to find the best information fast without having to wade through the sheer volume of fluff available online. Smart Reads combs through massive amounts of knowledge compiles the best into quick to read books on a variety of subjects.

We consider ourselves Smart Readers, not dummies. We know reading is smart. We're self taught. We like to learn a TON about a WIDE variety of topics. We have developed a love for books and we find intelligence attractive.

We found that each new topic we tried to learn about started with the challenge of finding the pieces of the puzzle that mattered most. It becomes a treasure hunt rather than an education.

Smart Reads wants to find the best of the best information for you. To condense it into a package that you can consume in an hour or less.  So you can read more books about more topics in less time.

# OUR MISSION

Smart Reads aims to accelerate the availability of useful information and will publish a high quality book on every major topic on amazon.

Smart Reads hopes to remove barriers to sharing by taking the copyright off everything we publish and donating it to the public domain. We hope other publishers and authors will follow our example.

Our goal is to donate $1,000,000 or more by 2020 to build over 2,000 schools by giving 5% of our net profit to Pencils of Promise.

We want to restore forests around the globe by planting a tree for every 10 physical books we sell and hope to plant over 100,000 trees by 2020.

Doesn't it feel good knowing that by educating yourself you are helping the world be a better place? We think so too...

Thanks for helping us help the world. You Smart Reader you...

Travis and the Smart Reads Team

# WHY I STARTED SMART READS

Every time I wanted to learn about something new I'd have to buy 20 books on the topic and spend way too long sorting through them and reading them all until I arrived at the big picture. Until I had enough perspectives to know who was just guessing, who was uninformed and who had stumbled upon something remarkable.

I wished someone else could just go in and figure that out for me and tell me what matters. That's how smart reads was born. I want smart reads to be a company that does all that research up front. Sorts through all the content that is available on each topic and pulls out the most up to date complete understanding, then have people smarter than me package the best wisdom in an easy to understand way in the least amount of words possible.

For example, I got a new puppy so I wanted to learn about dog training. I bought 14 different books about dog training and by the time I got through the first 5 and finally started getting the big picture on the best way to train my puppy she had grown up into a dog.

Yeah she's well behaved. She doesn't poop in the house. I can get her to sit and come when I call. But what if someone else went in and read all those books for me, found the underlying themes and picked out the best information that would give me the big picture and get me right to the point. And I'd only have to read one book instead of 15.

That would be amazing. I would save time. And maybe my dog would be rolling over, cleaning up after my kids and doing the dishes by now. That my friend, is the reason I started smart reads. Because I wanted a company I can trust to deliver me the best information in an easy to understand way that I can digest in under an hour. Because dog training is one of many subjects I want to master.

The quicker I can learn a wide variety of topics the sooner that information can begin playing a role in shaping my future. And none of us knows how long that future will be. So why not do everything we can to make the best of it and consume a ton of knowledge. And I figured all the better if I can also make a positive difference in the world.

That's why we're also building schools, planting trees and challenging ideas about copyright's place in today's world.  Because as a company we have to be doing everything we can to support the ecosystem that gives us all these beautiful places to read our books. Thanks for reading.

Travis

# Customers Who Bought This Customers Who Bought This Book Also Bought

*Thrive As An Empath: How to Protect Against Psychic Vampires and Leverage Your Special Gifts*

*Dealing With Anxiety: Modern Techniques for an Age Old Condition*

*Kundalini Awakening: Techniques To Raise Your Shakti Energy*

*Self-Esteem Supercharger: Build Self Worth and Find Your Inner Confidence*

*Meditation Magic: Free Yourself from Worry, Depression, Stress and Anxiety*

*How To Control Alcoholism: Proven Techniques to Stop Alcohol Abuse, Overcome Dependency, Break Addiction and Recover Your Life*

*Neuro Linguistic Programming: NLP Techniques for Hypnosis, Mind Control, Human Behavior, Relationships, Confidence*